Color My Mini Fruits! In Polish

By SOLA OLU TOTO

A Coloring and Activity Book For Kids!

A Coloring and Activity Book For Kids
That Inspires Confidence and Interactions!

ISBN-10: 1081683295

ISBN-13: 978-1-0816-8329-0

The pages of this coloring book are well suitable for crayons and colored pencils for kids
The coloring pages and activities herein, are designed so each child can find some tasks to do
at their unique ages. It is also great for framing, making of cute cards and bookmarks that can
be shared.

For school orders, bulk purchases, and more languages, please contact us via email
Contact: totoimprints@gmail.com.

Also check us out at: ToTo Imprints

ToTo Inspires Imprints
Publisher
www.totoinspires.me

Also Available:

This Book, **Color My Mini Fruits**, is also available in:

Polish

Swahili

German

Portuguese

French

Malagasy

Spanish

Yoruba

Javanese

Italian

Vietnamese

Kurdish

Xhosa

And over 45 languages.

www.totoinspires.me

Add your color to these unique series as you keep afresh your native languages in the lips of those precious young ones!

Great tool for creative expressions at home, schools, daycares, trips, afterschool programs and summer camps

Welcome To Color My Mini Fruits

This coloring book is a great way to spend quality time with your young ones. It has been specially designed to foster creative expressions, instill confidence and inspire interactions.

Add your color to these sets of fruits while your kids also learn to name and call items in your native language. A refreshing course for some parents, perhaps. Certainly, a curious adventure for others. This is an exciting way to learn while having fun. You can share your work of art with a special one or for social events.

Whether English is your primary language or not, the *Color My Mini Series* are uniquely designed to help prepare young ones to interact freely without limitations; whether at home, daycare, school or among others in life and social events. **Color My Mini Series** offers Early Learning through association, emphasis and creative expressions. My hope is to make accessible a tool that helps to minimize the withdrawal of young kids from interacting and speaking freely.

Through familiarity and association, we can help instill confidence early with each child. In addition, a native language should not be a limitation but a leverage. The more kids can identify and familiarize with these terms, the more freely they can be at expressing themselves. With simple illustrations, **Color My Mini Fruits** is designed for young kids. For complexity, please pick up the **My Mini Plus** for older kids with more activities and creative expressions.

Thank you,

Sola Olu ToTo
ToTo Inspires Imprints
www.totoinspires.me

About Polish Language

Polish is the official language of Poland.
Poland is a nation, located in Central Europe. It is the largest nation in Central Europe and the ninth (9ᵗʰ) largest country in Europe by land area. Polish is the second most spoken Slavic language after Russian; and the third most spoken language in U.K., after English and Welsh. Polish is often spoken at dinner time, which is traditionally eaten in the afternoon, about 1 or 2 p.m.

Did You Know?

Learning Languages: It is fun to learn about a foreign language. It helps you connect to your family heritage and learn something completely new. This can help you make more friends, make traveling fun, and be smart. Learning multiple languages is so much easier if you are still a kid. Experts believe kids who are exposed to more than one language tend to obtain greater focus, learn music easier and do better at tasks.

THIS BOOK BELONGS TO -

My name is:

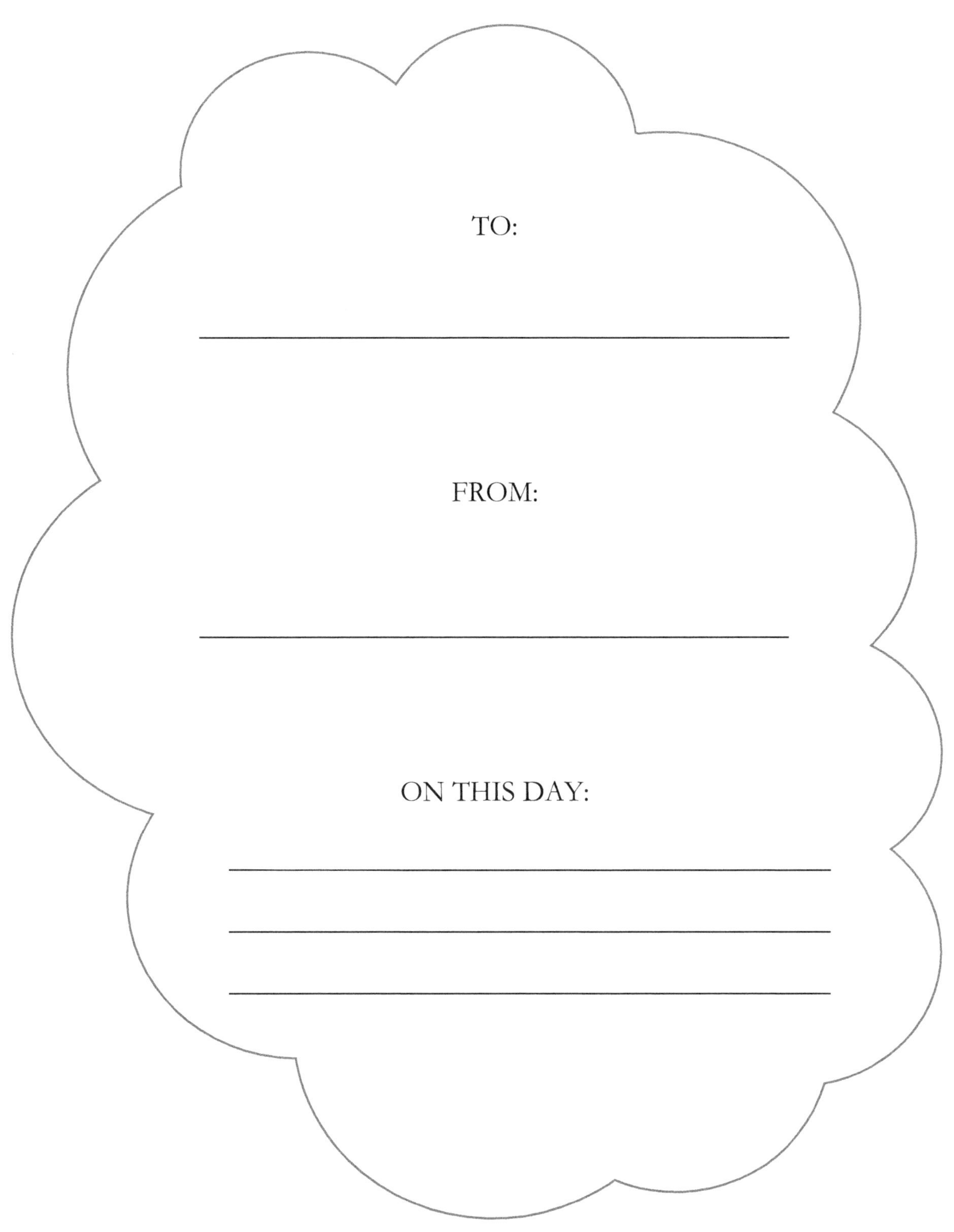
TO:

FROM:

ON THIS DAY:

Dzie dobry . Hello

Color my mini

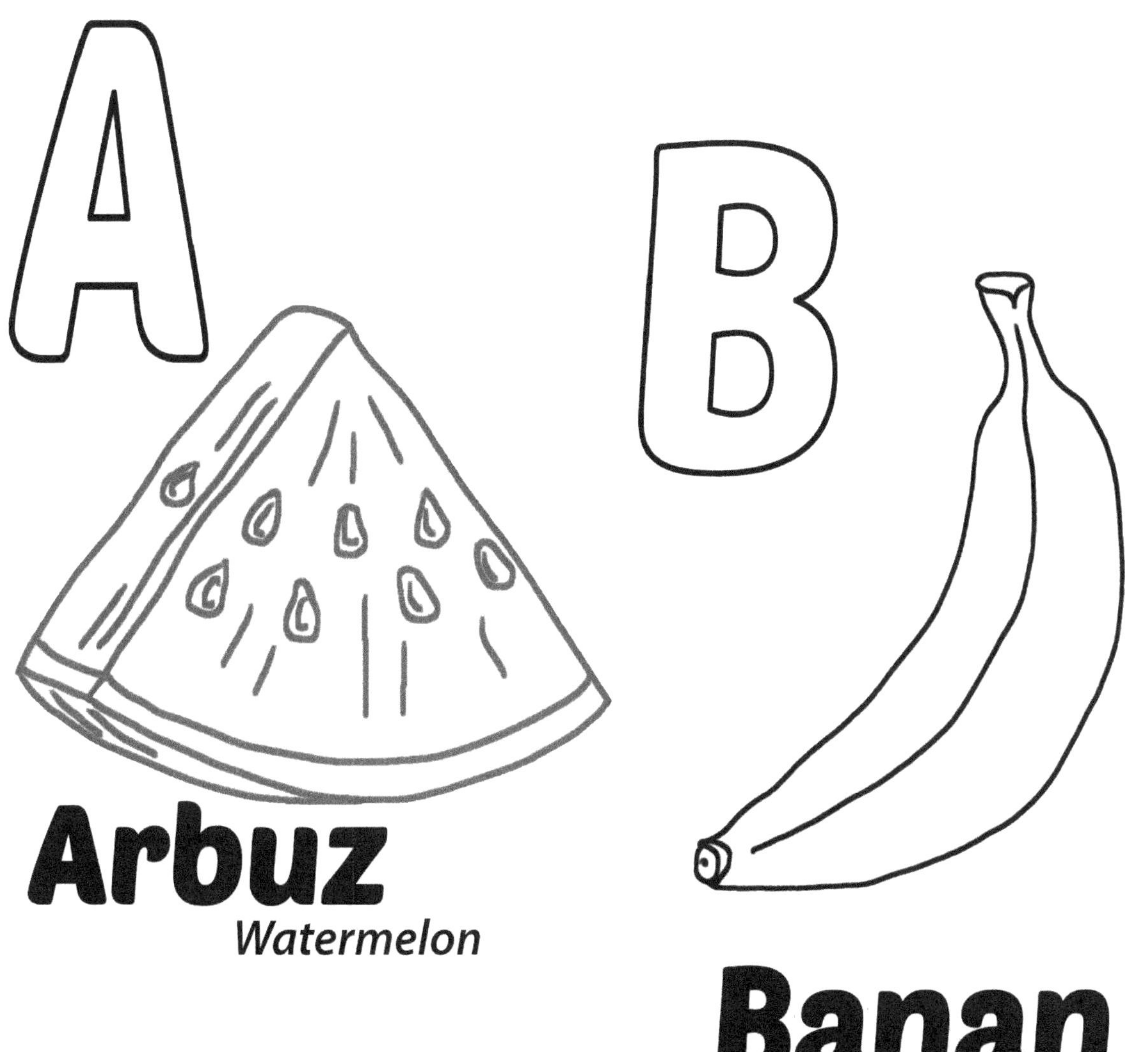

Arbuz
Watermelon

Banan
Banana

Makes me merry!

1 Wiśnia

2 Cherries

3 Wiśnie

I can
color

Mangowiec

Mango

Koloruj mój mini

Truskawki

Cytryny

Tylko trochę, proszę?
Just a little, please?

Blueberries, Blueberries,
Fall on me, a little
Till my hand is full
With just a little more!

S. Toto19

Powiedz dwa!

Gruszki
Pears

Wiśnie
Cherries

Truskawka
Strawberries

Brzoskwinia
Peaches

I can
color

Śliwka

Plum

I love
my
fruits!

Kocham moje owoce!

A ty?

So
I color!

I see, how many?

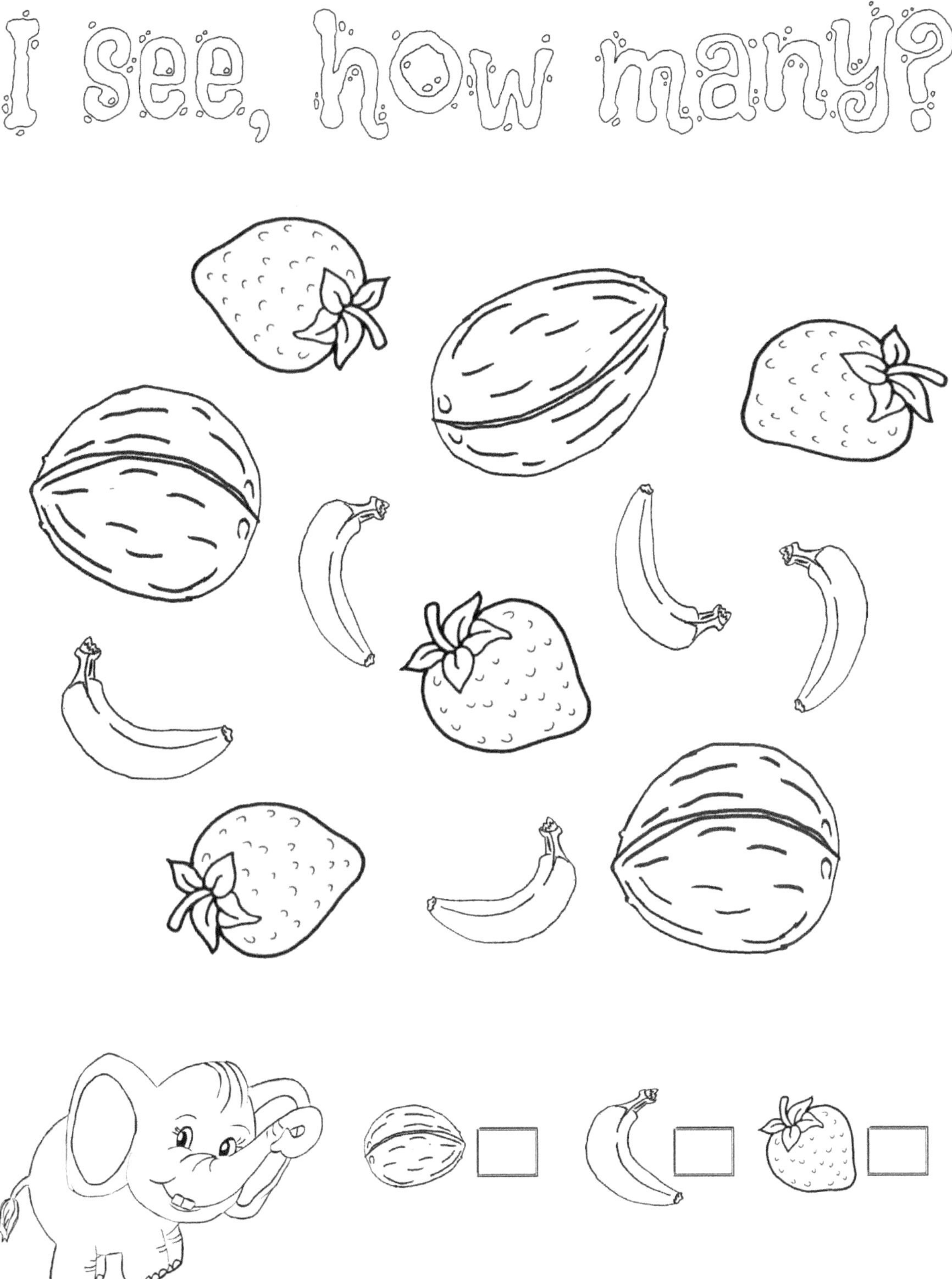

Can you
follow the
dots? It's a
fruit called

banan

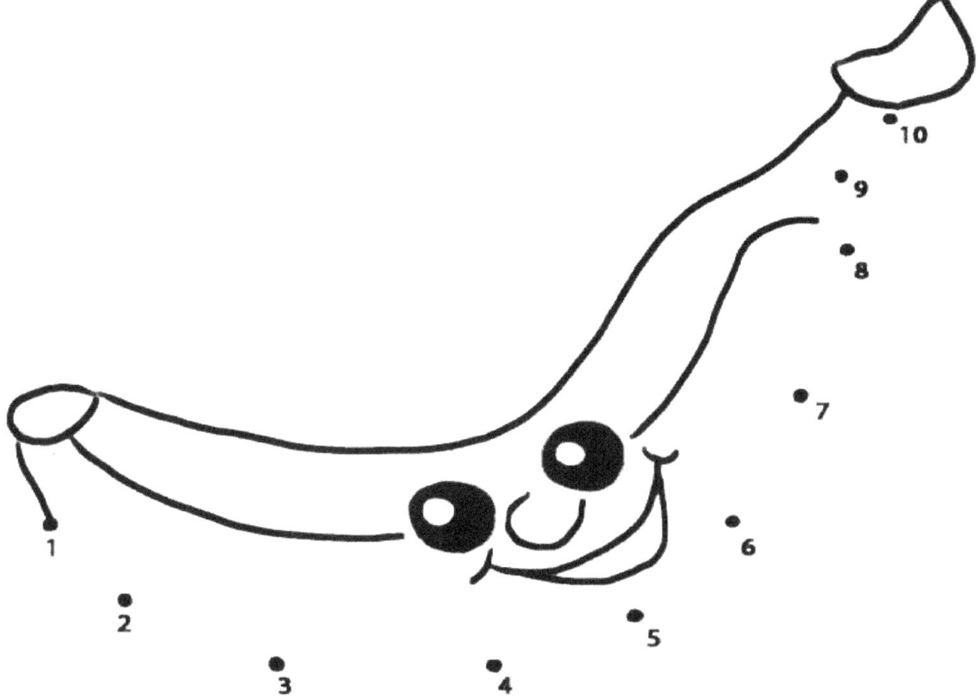

I love
my
fruits!!

Brzoskwinia

Peach

I can
color

Sharing . Dzielenie się

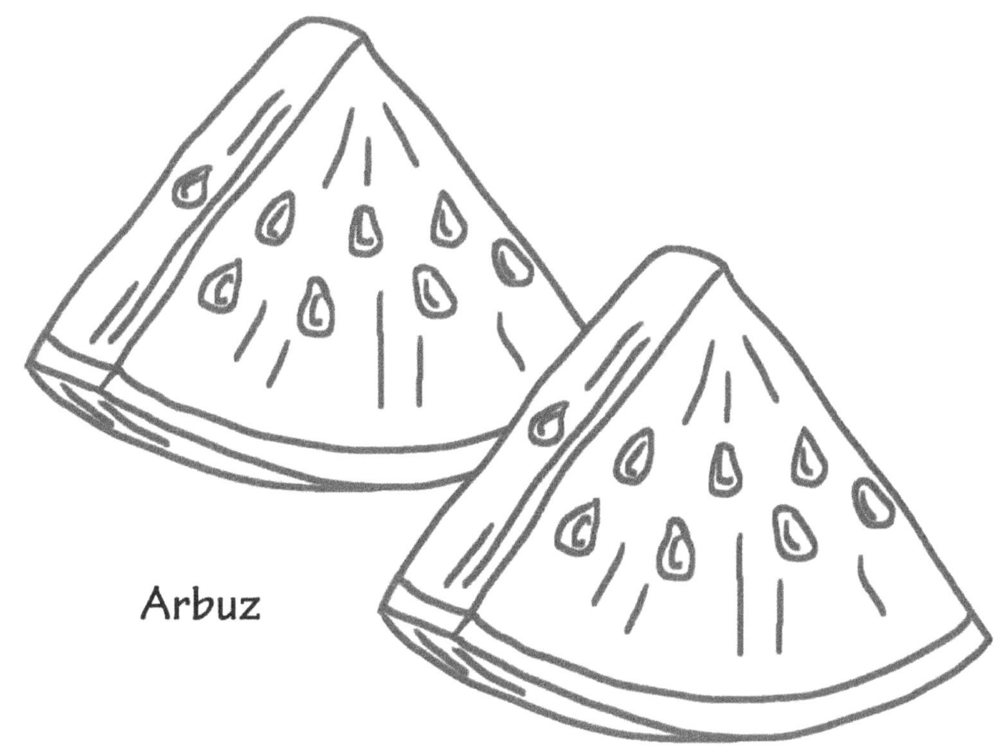

Arbuz

Czy mogę mieć kawałek arbuza?

Coconut

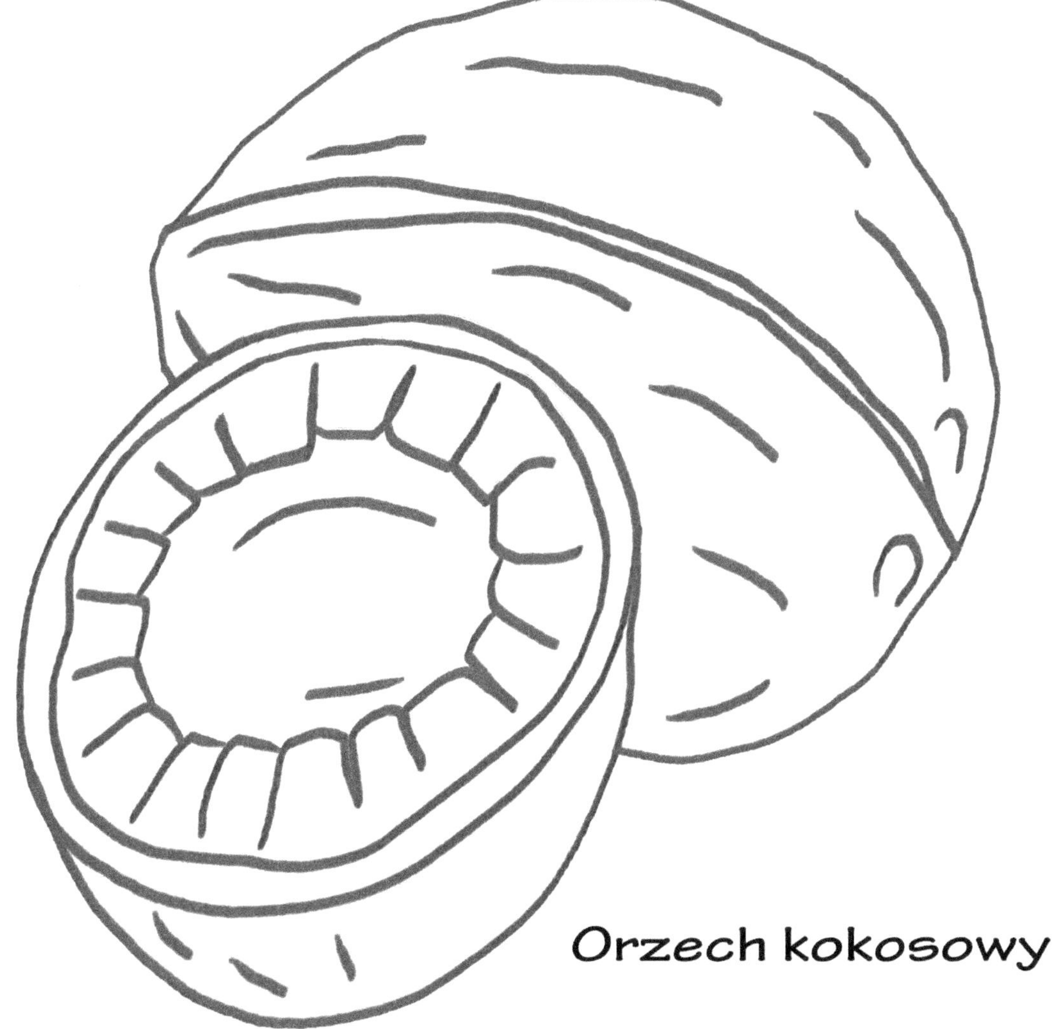

Orzech kokosowy

Banany

Bananas

Raz, Dwa,
Trzy.
I can

I love
my
fruits!

Koloruj mój mini

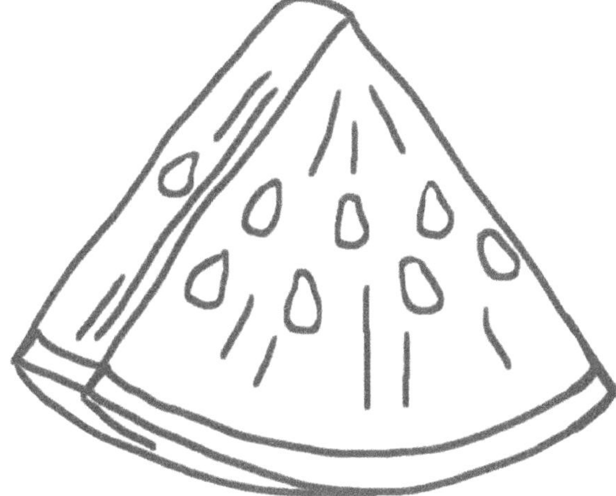

Arbuz
Watermelon

Pomarańczowy
Orange

Truskawka
Strawberry

Brzoskwinia
Peach

42

Sharing . Dzielenie się

Winogrona

Czy mogę mieć trochę winogron?

Dziękuję Ci

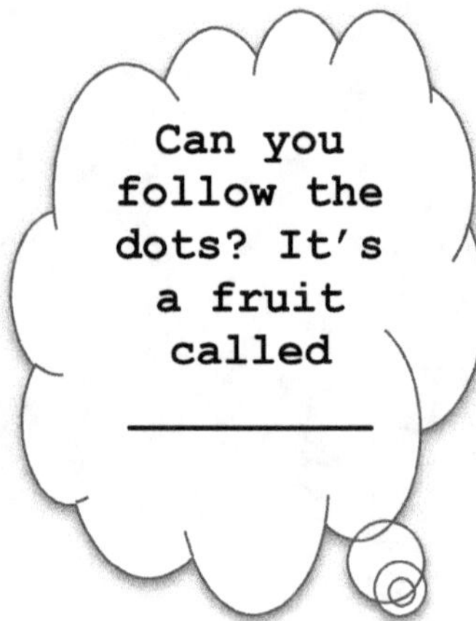
Can you
follow the
dots? It's
a fruit
called
____

GruszKa

1
2
3
15
4
5
14
6
13
7
12
8
11
10
9

I can
color!

Truskawki wszędzie
Strawberries everywhere

Znajd mnie, je li potrafisz!
Spot me if you can!

Coloring book

Mango
Mango

Winogrona
Grapes

Cytrynowy
Lemon

Jagody
Blueberry

Malina
Raspberry

Pomarańczowy
Orange

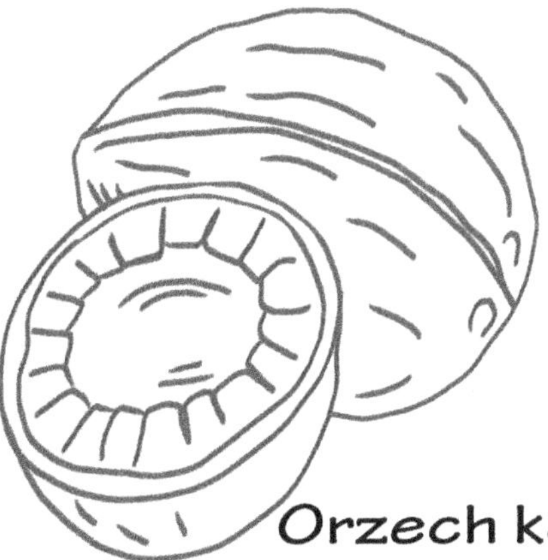

Orzech kokosowy
Coconut

Polsku i angielsku!

I know my fruits in Polish and English!

Znam moje owoce po polsku i angielsku!

Polish	**English**
Gruszka	Pear
Pomarańczowy	Orange
Jabłko	Apple
Banan	Banana
Wiśnia	Cherry
Brzoskwinia	Peach
Cytrynowy	Lemon
Arbuz	Watermelon
Truskawka	Strawberry
Malina	Raspberry
Orzech kokosowy	Coconut
Mangowiec	Mango
Borówka amerykańska	Blueberry
Śliwka	Plum

Koloruj mój mini

ABOUT THE AUTHOR

Sola Olu ToTo enjoys producing great inspiring books for children and adults alike. With a passion for cultures around the world; Sola's books instill excitements, courage and entertaining contents to foster a love for wits, creativity and global culture learning. Watch out for her upcoming book – "Patches!"

CONNECT WITH THE AUTHOR

Sola Olu ToTo loves to hear from you. You can connect with Sola with your inquiries and get updates on upcoming releases and promotions.

Booklife: https://booklife.com/profile/toto-imprints-33635

Twitter: https://twitter.com/TotoSola

Website: www.totoinspires.me

www.ingramcontent.com/pod-product-compliance
Lightning Source LLC
Chambersburg PA
CBHW081303130726
47998CB00010B/2905